WILHELM HANSEN EDITION NO. 3797

J. S. Bach

TOCCATA and FUGUE

in d minor

for Piano by Carl Tausig

BMV No. 565

Edition Wilhelm Hansen, Copenhagen

TOCCATA.

26506

ISBN 87 7455 289 9

4

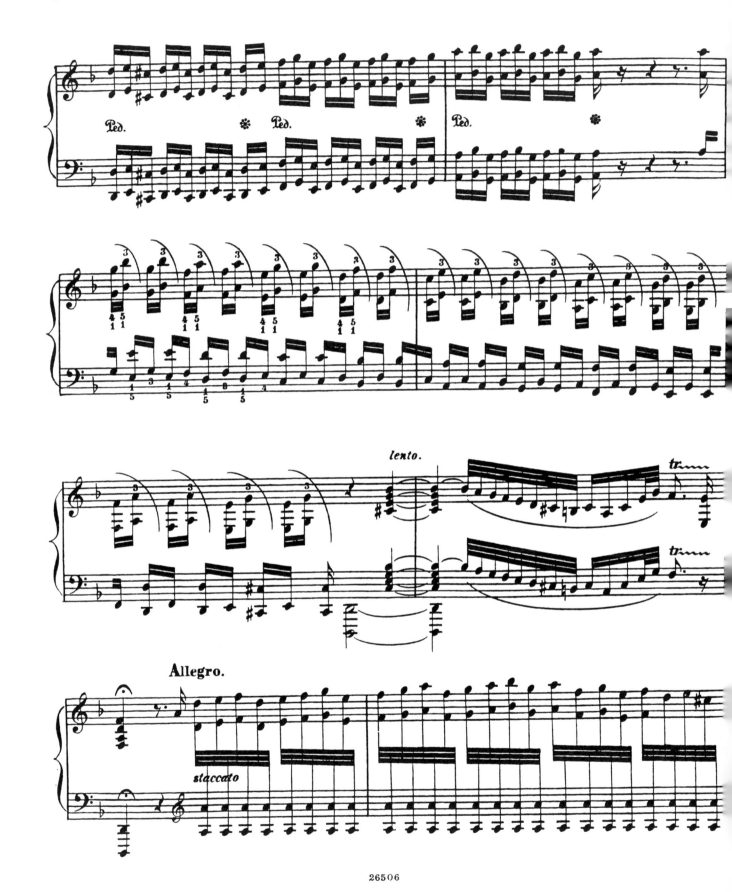

26506

6

26506

FUGE.

Allegro.

8

Ossia piu facilé.

cresc.

26506

26506

14